The Short Book of Suicide: A Simple Explanation For Why You Should Not End Your Life or Engage in Self-Harm

Chapter 1: About Suicide

What Is Suicide?

Suicide is the intentional killing of oneself. People refer to suicide when someone has taken their own life. Other commonly used phrases people use to describe suicide include: committing suicide, killing oneself, ending their lives, or passing away at "one's own hand."

In general, it is best not to say "committing suicide" or "committed suicide. Survivors of suicide loss say "died by suicide." It is important to respect survivors.

In many cultures, death by suicide is considered a sin or is seen as shameful. In some states throughout the United States, suicide is a felony crime. Though it may technically be against the law to die by suicide, states generally do not enforce the law.

General Statistics

Throughout the world, suicide rates have increased by approximately 60 percent over the past 45 years. Studies have shown that suicide is the leading cause of death in the world. The World Health Organization estimates that approximately 1,000,000 individuals in the world die by suicide every year. That is one death every 40 seconds.

Why Suicide?

There is no easy answer to this question. Understanding why someone would decide to die by suicide is very complex. It often involves psychological, social, biological, cultural, and environmental factors. Some consider it one of the most perplexing human behaviors ever studied. Often there is no understandable answer.

Individuals who are considering suicide are often assuming the worst outcome in their lives and thus, in their mind, it makes sense to consider suicide. But they are wrong—so very wrong. Someone who is considering suicide is experiencing clouded judgment. They are not thinking clearly. Getting help can help to avert a tragedy. There are many possible reasons why someone would take her own life. Some of the main reasons are listed below.

Don't Want To Suffer

Many people think about suicide when they are in severe psychological pain or are living with what they perceive to be intolerable conditions. They may believe that ending their life is a way to end their pain. They feel as though it will "all be over" when they were no longer alive. They just want their pain to end.

Individuals experiencing chronic physical pain may also see suicide as a way to end their suffering. If someone feels as though they can no longer tolerate physical pain they may feel as though not living is the better option.

Believe Suicide Is Their Only Option

Many individuals, possibly due to psychological problems, have difficulty judging reality correctly. For instance, individuals with depression often feel hopeless. They may believe that there is no solution to their problem. They may feel despondent and can't envision a change in their emotional status. They inaccurately believe that their life will never change. That distorted view of reality leads them to conclude the only option is to end their lives.

Lack of Coping Skills

People may contemplate suicide for many other reasons but often it may be because they lack effective coping skills to deal with difficult life situations. This is particularly true for teenagers who often have yet to develop these necessary life skills. If some aspect of their life is stressful, not having the skills to decrease their stress or to solve the problem is frustrating. This frustration may lead them to believe that there's no solution to the problem and thus they consider suicide. This is especially true if an individual feels feel as though they have no one they can confide in or gain support from. Having a lack of support could make someone feel isolated and lonely.

Mental Health Disorder

Some studies have shown that having a mental illness is strongly associated with suicide. Some reports show that up to 90% of individuals who die by suicide have a diagnosable mental illness. Conflicting studies, on the other hand, have shown that there are people who have died by suicide and who do not have a mental health disorder.

The most common mental health disorders associated with suicide are schizophrenia, alcohol use disorders, and depression. Having one of those mental health diagnoses does not mean that someone will die by suicide but it may increase the likelihood of a suicide death.

Impulsivity

Impulsivity means acting without much forethought. It may involve acting on a feeling or a thought without considering the consequences. With regard to suicide, some research has shown that impulsivity plays an important role in suicide attempts. Among individuals who have attempted suicide and who have survived, many say they attempted suicide during an acute crisis. They acted very quickly without much thought. People attempting suicide are not thinking clearly and can become fixated on the idea of ending their lives. Research indicates that having a lethal weapon stored in a lockbox can help put the needed time in between an emotional reaction and a decision about death. Lockboxes save lives.

Risk Factors of Suicide

Some of the most common risk factors for suicide include the
following:

- Having a current or past history of suicidal ideation or
  behavior;
- the availability of and access to lethal means of harm
  (including firearms and other deadly weapons);
- history of or exposure to trauma or abuse;
- family history of suicide;
- the use of alcohol or drugs;
- lacking significant relationships and support;
- being socially isolated;
- having a chronic physical illness;
- experiencing chronic or disabling pain;
- difficulty coping with life problems; and
- lacking access to health and social services

Having one or more of the risk factors above does not mean that
someone will attempt suicide. It may mean that they are at an
increased likelihood of attempting suicide. The two strongest
predictors of suicidal behavior are having a current or past history
of such behavior and having the availability or access to lethal
means of harm.

Methods of Suicide

According to research the most common methods of suicide
include poisoning by drugs, jumping, firearms, poisoning by means
other than drugs, jumping or lying before a moving object,
hanging, and drowning. In the United States, the two most
common methods of suicide are the use of a firearm and jumping
from a high place. It is generally believed that what individuals have
access to influences the method that they choose.

Men who attempt suicide are more likely to choose a violent or lethal method when compared to women. Men generally have higher rates of completed suicide than women. Men tend to have a higher risk of using firearms or hanging when compared to women. They also have a lower risk of using poisoning by drugs, drowning, or jumping.

Chapter 2: Why Suicide is the Wrong Answer

With the very rare exception of assisted suicide related to death with dignity laws, nothing, no plan that leads you to consider suicide as an option can be the correct plan. There are many, many reasons why you should not end your life. Some of them are listed below.

Unfairness To Your Family

The loss that your family will experience upon your suicide will be devastating. It is truly a family tragedy. Your family will suffer immensely. Having a family member who dies by suicide also increases the likelihood that other family members will also die by suicide. By ending your life, you are undoubtedly negatively impacting your family.

It is common for members of the family to blame themselves for your suicide. Even if it is unwarranted, they may feel guilty for your death. They may blame themselves for not "having done enough."

Survivors have also reported feeling as though the loved one's decision to end his or her life was their fault. Some have reported feeling "unloved" or believing things such as "they must not have loved me enough because if so, they would not have done this to me."

Anger is a common reaction as well. Family members may feel resentful for having to deal with the emotional aftermath of a suicide. For those reasons and many others, death by suicide is very unfair to your family.

Your Life Can Improve & There is Help Available

Problems are a part of life. We all experience them but your challenge might be that you lack coping skills to navigate life problems. Counseling could help. Coping skills can be learned.

Individuals who are considering suicide have lost hope. They don't believe that their life can change. It is a mistake to assume that your life will not improve. It has for many people and it can for you too.

Research about individuals who have attempted suicide and who have survived is very revealing. Many thought that their lives would never improve which is what led them to consider suicide in the first place.

Interestingly, those who have survived their attempts are thankful that they lived. They realized that even though they experienced very low points in life, there were happy times too. They were lucky enough to have survived to see their lives improve. Many of those who survived their suicide attempts, felt obligated to spread this message to prevent others from making the same mistake they did. They wanted people to know that with time, things can get better.

Studies show that people who have attempted suicide and survived are glad that they did not die. They had difficulty envisioning an end to their suffering and incorrectly thought that suicide was the answer to their problems. Having survived their suicide attempt, they realized that their problems were solvable and their feelings of hopelessness eventually passed.

The most moving examples of why suicide is wrong can be found in a 2008 *New York Times* article called "The Urge to End It All." The article recounts the lives of individuals who attempted suicide and survived. The individuals featured in the article reveal that they never really wanted to die. They just wanted their pain to stop. Attempting suicide was their maladaptive response to their stressful life circumstances. Each person featured in the article was grateful to have survived and now realize that their problems were solvable. None of them have thought about suicide again. They were thankful to have survived.

Dr. Viktor Frankl, the author of the best-selling book *Man's Search For Meaning*, shared a similar view of suicide. Like the individuals who survived their suicide attempts, Dr. Frankl's patients repeatedly told him how happy they were that they did not successfully die by suicide.

He also noticed that before their suicide attempts, individuals who attempted suicide and who survived reported feeling frustrated with not having an immediate solution to the problem. They later realized that even if there wasn't an immediate solution, eventually, they were able to solve their problems. Dr. Frankl says:

"I explain to such a person that patients have repeatedly told me how happy they were that the suicide attempt had not been successful; weeks, months, years later, they told me, it turned out that there was a solution to their problem, an answer to their question, a meaning to their life. Even if things only take such a good turn in one of a thousand cases," my explanation continues, "who can guarantee that in your case it will not happen one day, sooner or later?... You have to survive in order to see that day dawn."

Individuals who are considering suicide are assuming the worst outcome and thus in their mind, it makes sense to consider suicide. But they are wrong. Someone who is considering suicide is experiencing clouded judgment. They are not thinking clearly. Getting help can help to avert a tragedy.

Throughout life, there are many "ups and downs." There will be good periods and there will be bad periods. It is that way for everyone: rich or poor, celebrity or non-celebrity, young or old, etc.

To handle the inevitable stresses of life, one needs to possess coping skills. The fact that you are considering suicide as a way to deal with your pain likely means that you do not possess these necessary coping skills. However, you can develop them.

Your emotional pain may be preventing you from believing that there is hope and that things can change. Your life can become better. Realize that you might not be thinking clearly due to your emotional pain.

Try to see what can be learned from individuals who have attempted suicide and who have survived and who are thankful to have survived. Below is a true story of such a survivor.

AJ was 13 years old when he began having problems. He had been misbehaving. He robbed a gas station. His mother married a man with whom he did not get along. AJ drank to cope with his emotional pain.

At the age of 16, his stepfather kicked him out of the house. He then went to live with a friend. While at the friend's home, he took a gun from their gun cabinet and went outside, and shot himself in the face. He shot off most of his face. He is barely recognizable.

At the time that he attempted suicide, he could see no point in living. He survived and he is now blind. Despite being blind, he's thankful to have survived.

One might think that AJ would have later tried to end his life but he did not. He is glad to have survived.

AJ begs people to reconsider suicide. He realized that life can improve even when it feels like it can't. AJ has this advice for those considering suicide:

"If we just step back and strive towards tomorrow, it will get better…And the day after that will be better than the day before. So never give up. You don't know how many people you're going to hurt by leaving them behind."

James Giles

James Giles was an addict for 18 years. He saw no hope. In October 2000, he climbed a utility tower and jumped. He never expected to survive the incident.

"My mother and my grandmother were standing over me crying. I'd never seen them in that condition before and that is really when the realization of 18 years of me doing drugs — how selfish, inconsiderate, and self-centered I was," he said. "I never thought about the consequences it was having on my family, my loved ones, people who were praying, people sitting up nights wondering where I was or what I was doing, if I was dead or in jail for killing someone — I came to the realization I was doing it to myself and to my family."

There is another way, believe it or not," he said. *"You've just got to get sick and tired of being sick and tired. You've got to come to the realization that you have to take life by the horns and live it…"*

Kevin Hines had been suffering tremendously from the symptoms of bipolar disorder. He pretended to be taking his medications and following a treatment plan but he wasn't. He was getting worse. He then concluded, after hiding his symptoms for months, that he was not okay.

"I didn't know how to cope," he said. *"I didn't want to die, but because of my psychosis, I believed that I had to die. I thought that everybody hated me, they were just pretending to be nice to me."*

He decided to end his life. It made him feel peaceful. Hines says that many people who decide to end their lives feel at peace with their decision. They believe that their pain will be gone. He climbed over the rail of the Golden Gate Bridge and jumped. He explains:

"The millisecond I hit freefall, when my hands and feet left the rail, I said, 'What have I just done? I don't want to die. God, please save me," he said. *"People get shocked into reality and they realize immediately they've made a mistake and I knew I made a mistake."*

Hines survived a fall that very few people ever survive. His life is now devoted to preventing suicide. He says:

"If you're considering suicide right now, if you've ever thought about suicide and it haunts you — suicide is never the solution for any problem. But when you feel that way, you have to know you're not alone, there are millions of people who have thought about suicide," Hines said. *"Hope exists, and a future, while living with a mental health issue or a suicidal thought, exists. It's not easy. You have to work hard."*

Your Suffering May Not End

Many people assume that if they end their life their suffering will end but we do not know if that is true. By assuming that your suffering will end by ending your life, you are essentially saying that you know what happens after we die. No one knows what happens after we die.

In the book, *Life After Life* Dr. Raymond Moody discusses several accounts of individuals who had "hellish" near-death experiences after a suicide attempt. They believed they had experienced hell. Those accounts were in stark contrast to the individuals who did not purposefully attempt to end their lives (i.e., died by accident) and who had near-death experiences. Generally, those latter experiences were positive and inspirational. In fact, I would highly encourage you to read those stories because even reading about them can be transformative.

Consider the case of Matthew Dovel. He claims to have had two near-death experiences, one in which he experienced heaven another in which he experienced "hell." At 12 years old, Matthew accidentally drowned in a swimming pool. He described having a very loving near-death experience. He believed that he had met his "Creator."

Years later, after living a very troubled and unhappy life, he wanted to relive his earlier near-death experience and end his suffering. He decided to die by suicide but ultimately, he survived. His second near-death experience was very different than his first. He described spending three days in hell. It was a terrifying and awful experience. He was thankful to have survived his suicide attempt and realized that he had made a major mistake.

His latter near-death experience led to the development of the International Suicide Prevention public charity program. He has since dedicated his life to suicide prevention. Perhaps he was motivated by the hellish near-death experience after his suicide attempt. His experience and the experience of others may have been a sign that death by suicide would result in more suffering in the "afterlife" rather than less.

Relatedly, the *Divine Comedy*, the work by Dante Alighieri from the 1300s, provides some food for thought about suicide. In one of his most famous poems, Dante's *Inferno*, he describes the nine circles of hell. Individuals who died by suicide were considered to have engaged in violence directed at themselves. Dante placed them in the seventh circle of hell because, as he describes it, they deliberately courted death and wasted the gift of life. In essence, they gave up the privilege of self-determination. They did not use rational thought to choose how to respond to the difficulties of life.

By giving up their ability to reason and use rational thought, they were punished severely. They were placed in gloomy wood to live in eternity as grubby shrubs. As grubby shrubs, they could not move or speak or do anything. Guarding them were harpies, who were described as half-bird, half-woman beings. The harpies would feast on the leaves of the grubby shrubs who would complain about the pain they had to endure. As noted by David Bruce in his discussion guide of Dante's *Inferno*, "as human beings, we have free will, and we can choose how we respond to a disaster. We can give in to discouragement and commit suicide or we can respond in a more courageous way."

Though Dante's *Inferno* is a work of fiction, his warnings about hell in the afterlife should make one reconsider suicide as an option. It should never be an option. If there is such a place as hell, no one should be willing to risk a life of endless suffering for all of eternity. The most rational response to the problem of suicidal thinking is to seek help.

Another Dimension to Life

Recounted in the book *The Map of Heaven: How Science, Religion, and Ordinary People Are Proving The Afterlife* by Eben Alexander, M.D., he recounts how biologist Alister Hardy studied the "inner" experiences of more than 3,000 people. He described the following:

"At certain times in our lives many people have had specific, deeply felt, transcendental experiences which have made them all aware of the presence of this power... It occurs to children, to atheists and agnostics, and it usually induces in the person concerned a conviction that the everyday world is not the whole of reality: that there is another dimension to life."

You might try meditation to attempt to encourage these inner experiences, which could have a strong, positive effect on you. Research consistently shows the many positive benefits of meditation.

Why You Should Get Help

Suicide is always the wrong answer. In every case, it is a tragedy. It is particularly tragic because there is help available.

People may contemplate suicide for many reasons but fundamentally it's due to the emotional pain that they feel and likely because they have not yet developed the appropriate coping skills. The good news is, these skills can be learned.

As noted above, many individuals who attempted suicide and who survived were thankful to have lived. They are living witnesses to the truth, which is that there will be problems in life, and those problems will not always have an immediate solution but eventually they can be resolved. You must remain alive in order to see those problems resolved "...in order to see that day dawn" as Frankl would say.

Another important reason why you should seek help is that suicide is a particularly harsh tragedy for the family. Your family will suffer without you. Death by suicide will forever scar members of your family. As mentioned earlier, it could increase the likelihood that another member of your family will die by suicide.

Consider the case of Daisy Coleman, who was featured in the *Netflix* documentary *"Audrey & Daisy."* It was a harrowing story about sexual assault. In August 2020, Daisy took her life. She was discovered after her mother called the police to do a welfare check.

Her mother, Melinda, said that Daisy was her best friend and that she was an amazing daughter. She did not think she could live life without her.

Sadly, just four months later, Melinda Coleman also died by suicide. Melinda had also lost her son Tristan in 2018 in the crash. We'll never know what role losing her daughter to suicide played in her decision to end her own life, but all likelihood, it was a major factor.

Having The Right Attitude About Life & Not Being Impatient

It is important to be patient in life. Impatient people want things when they want them. They often become angry when things don't go their way.

People who are impatient either don't accept reality or are unwilling to accept reality. For instance, the impatient and quick-tempered person sitting in an unexpected traffic jam will be seething with anger because they have been delayed. Anger in that situation stems from their inability to accept reality coupled with the perceived expectation of things going as planned.

We must accept the fact that things will not always go our way. There will be disappointments, annoyances, and unpleasant developments in life. We must come to expect them. They will happen to all of us. The proper response to these inevitabilities is to develop the proper coping skills to deal with these situations when they arise.

If that does not help, there are several ways to address this problem. The most effective method of treatment would be to see a therapist who specializes in anger management. Therapy will likely focus on the development of new coping skills and new ways of thinking about life situations.

Also, consider taking an anger management class. A well-designed anger management program can be immensely effective. You can learn how to properly express your anger in a healthy, constructive manner. You'll learn that while you can't control your feelings you can control how you react to them.

A self-help approach involves educating yourself about anger. This would include reading anger management books and workbooks.

Some People Think It is All About Attention. It's Not!

No one would willingly choose to experience negative thoughts. Those thoughts and images are essentially your brain playing tricks on you. It's unfair, unpleasant, and frightening. It will stop but it can take time.

No one chooses to be depressed, just like no one chooses to be diabetic. Depression *happens* to people. You're not to blame, nor is it within your expertise as a layperson to know how to cure yourself. Professional help is often required and that's okay.

Never feel like you are a bother to your doctor or mental health provider. You are not. If you are a bother to your doctor, then they should find a new occupation. No good therapist would ever be upset with you providing the very information that they need to do their very best work. Be honest and forthright.

Not Happy With Life

Let's say that you are not very happy with your life the way it is now. People make a big mistake when they reflect upon their life and say "I should be happy." Often what they mean by "I should be happy" is that, by normal societal goals and values, they have had success and thus "should be happy."

It is enough to say that with all the success, fortune, and fame that they have acquired they are not happy. Many people would argue over why they are unhappy. Some would say it's a chemical imbalance, others would say they have had a poor childhood, others would say they are cognitively incorrect, others would say that they are not self-actualizing or individuating and yet others would say yet other things.

It is my deepest belief that a happy or satisfying or meaningful life is the goal and destiny of each individual. The goal is rarely achieved without much diligent effort. The goal is never reached if it is not recognized or valued.

When You Don't Feel Like Living Anymore

This may be a sign of depression. When people are depressed it's difficult for them to envision their life improving. A sort of tunnel vision develops making it difficult to believe that change is possible. In that way, depression can stifle positive growth and change.

Individuals who are depressed also perceive others as being much happier than they really are. They assume that everyone else is happy and is flourishing. They assume that they are the only ones who are unhappy since obviously everyone looks happy. For some, it becomes the proof that they are a "loser" which ultimately serves to fuel their depression. However, when we look at others, we need to remember that we can only see the outside. Most people carefully control the "outside" that is public and manipulate that appearance to give the best possible impression. Simply put, they hide their doubts and fears and often their true feelings.

Many people also wait too long to seek treatment. It may be because they don't recognize that good treatment is available. Perhaps it's because they erroneously feel that they should be able to help themselves without the assistance of professionals. Don't make those mistakes in judgment. It is important to realize that psychological pain can be eliminated from your life. It's often a matter of finding the right therapist and/or combination of medications and treatments.

Sometimes, people want a "quick fix." They expect medication to essentially cure their psychological problems. They don't want to take the time to thoroughly address their issues in psychotherapy. This is a mistake. Medication can reduce disorder symptoms but it's generally recommended that psychological problems be treated with both medicine and psychotherapy.

Carl Jung believed that depression was simply the conscious mind being forced into closer alignment with the unconscious mind, where the roots of consciousness and the beginning of the pathways of consciousness exist. This pathway of growth, he termed individuation. It is similar to Abraham Maslow's concept of self-actualization. Both topics are worthy of personal study.

Many believe that depression stems from not having meaning in one's life. Most famous among them is Dr. Viktor Frankl, the psychiatrist who originated logotherapy. Logotherapy is essentially the process of discovering a meaning or purpose in one's life. That meaning of life will be different for each individual. He believed that individuals may feel overall unhappiness or dissatisfaction with their life if they have not found that meaning.

What If You Already Tried Therapy?

You may have chosen the wrong therapist. It is also possible that you might be misperceiving your therapists' responses to you. Be very upfront with your therapist. Be frank. Tell your therapist how you feel and why you feel that way. Never hold anything back from your therapist. When you withhold information from your therapist you are asking them to be more detective than therapist. It might not be appropriate to tell a friend all that you feel. It might not be appropriate to tell your dentist all that you are feeling but is very, very appropriate to tell your therapist. What I am saying is that your therapist is very unique. They deal with emotion. You should share all of your thoughts and feelings with your therapist. If you feel pain in your tooth, don't share that with your therapist. If you feel fear of going to the dentist to have your tooth fixed, share that with your therapist. They will help you overcome that fear. Change therapists if necessary and don't stop trying until you find someone you like.

How will you know if you are being helped in therapy? You should feel as though the therapist "gets it." You should leave every session feeling a little better. You should feel a connection with your therapist. You should feel that the therapist understands you.

It is also important to understand that therapy can take years to be fully effective. Don't give up. Many of the problems, that individuals are dealing with, are complex and may stem from childhood.

Two great self-help books include *The Road Less Traveled* by M. Scott Peck and *Man's Search For Meaning* by Viktor Frankl. These books could be considered to be timeless in that they contain a great deal of enduring wisdom and address a wide variety of problems including anger, depression, anxiety, and suicidal ideation.

What is the Purpose of Life?

When you question the purpose of life, you are basically asking does life have a purpose? Is it a temporary inconvenience, of no relative value, that simply delays you from that of ultimate value: heaven? Have you asked a good question or a silly trivial question? The answer is: you have asked a very good question that many philosophers have asked before you. It is such a good question that you should not be given a trivial answer. The question is of such ultimate complexity that you should not be satisfied with a trite or dogmatic answer.

Anyone who offers you an answer, is in essence suggesting that they know as much as God or knows the mind or purpose of God. Can mere humans or science, know the mind of God? I mean, after all, we don't know where we came from, we don't know why we're here, we don't know what we're supposed to be doing and we don't know where will be going (when we die and we will die). Science has told us much about creation. Science can take us back to the Big Bang but no further. What science tells us about creation and the Big Bang is simply unimaginable. Science tells us that there was nothing; no matter, no space, no time, no light.

Imagine, no space, all things at the same point. Imagine no time, no before, no after, no "right" now. I say imagine but really what I mean to say, is try to imagine because I know full well that it is impossible to imagine. However, it is essential to try.

Though no one can give you a good answer, including our best quantum physicists and cosmologists, it is essential to understand the complexity of the question. There was a time that science would laugh at the idea of heaven or the survival of death. Today science proposes a reality that is so amazingly complex, that it may well be beyond human comprehension. Science talks about our existing in many dimensions, beyond the three of which we are aware, height, width, length (and time, the possible fourth). Science says we exist in those dimensions but we are unable to perceive them. Though we can't perceive them we can prove their existence, mathematically. At least that is the contention of many quantum physicists. Perhaps even more impressively, science suggests the existence of a "multiverse," of which our universe is just one of an infinite number of others. Each universe has its own laws of physics and each is different. Science also says that perhaps we exist, you and I, in each of those universes. Science also says that time, may simply be an illusion, not real at all.

As science becomes more advanced, as it discovers more knowledge, it allows for the existence of God, of heaven, of the survival of death.

Not everyone thinks about the philosophical questions or about quantum physics or about cosmology but those that do, are certainly not among the unintelligent. They are thoughts of an insightful mind.

Why Do I Have A Difficult Life?

With regard to living a difficult life, Dr. Brian Weiss, who has written a great deal about reincarnation and spiritual matters, said the following:

"Sometimes a soul chooses a particularly challenging lifetime in order to accelerate its spiritual progress, or as an act of love to help, guide, and nourish

others who are also going through a similarly difficult lifetime. A hard life is not a punishment, but rather an opportunity."

Dr. Viktor Frankl, a psychiatrist, and Holocaust survivor believes that struggling in life is the norm rather than the exception. Expect to suffer, learn effective ways of coping with it, and attempt to find meaning in that suffering. Dr. Frankl also suggested that one should, if possible, attempt to utilize negative life struggles in positive ways. He referred to this concept as tragic optimism. Tragic optimism essentially means turning something negative into something positive.

When Someone You Love Is Suicidal

For a layperson, the ability to help a suicidal friend or family member is almost non-existent. Yes, you love them more than anyone else, but what skill do you have as a therapist? You love them more than their therapist but you simply lack the education and training necessary to deal with their problem.

You would never think of performing surgery on a loved one, not because you don't love them sufficiently but because you simply lack the ability and experience of a surgeon. It's obvious to most people that without the skill and knowledge of a surgeon it would be foolish and perhaps deadly to perform surgery on someone you love.

Without many years of education and experience, it would be just as foolish to attempt to do counseling with someone you love. If you have a friend or a family member who is having a mental problem and you want to know what you can do for them, encourage them to seek the help of professionals.

Chapter 3: Cutting as Self-Injurious Behavior

Why Do People Cut Themselves?

In the psychiatric literature, cutting is categorized as non-suicidal self-injury. Non-suicidal self-injury essentially refers to the purposeful engagement of harming the body without the intention of ending one's life. In other words, an individual who cuts is likely not intending to die. In general, cutting is a sign that someone is experiencing significant psychological suffering.

Cutting is one form of self-injury but other common types include burning, banging one's head on the wall, severely scratching one's body, or inserting objects under the skin. Particular areas of the body are targeted for self-injury include arms, hands, wrists, thighs, and the stomach.

There are many reasons that people might cut themselves. Read on to find out about the most common reasons and to learn about the general profile of someone who cuts.

Who Cuts?

Cutting tends to begin around the ages of 13 and 14. Individuals who cut generally do so as adolescents or young adults. Studies have shown that approximately 15% of adolescents and young adults in the United States and Canada report cutting. Some studies have reported that up to 45% of adolescents have reported engaging in self-injury at some point during their lives. The majority of people who engage in cutting will eventually stop.

Individuals who have mental health disorders such as anorexia, bulimia, panic disorder, obsessive-compulsive disorder, and borderline personality disorders are more likely to engage in self-injurious behavior when compared to individuals without those disorders.

Informal reports from mental health and other health professionals have shown that there is a general belief that self-injury has dramatically increased in the past 10 to 20 years. Unfortunately, there is no historical data to support that assertion.

Both men and women engage in self-injury but women are more likely to engage in cutting. Caucasians engage in self-injury and a higher rate than non-Caucasians. No one knows why that is the case.

Individuals tend to cut themselves when they're alone and when they are experiencing negative thoughts. This may include feeling as though they made a mistake, feeling bad about themselves, feeling angry, or having a traumatic memory.

Other Possible Reasons Why People Cut Themselves

A Belief That They Deserve To Suffer

Some individuals engage in cutting because they believe that they deserve to suffer. Feeling that one deserves to suffer is often connected to perceived wrongdoing. An individual may believe that they need to punish themselves for what see as improper behavior or a mistake.

For instance, you fought with your partner and said hurtful things that you feel guilty about. What you said to your partner hurt them badly. As a way to punish yourself, you cut yourself. You may be thinking that you should suffer because of your mistake. You made your partner suffer and thus may believe that you deserve to suffer too.

In another instance, perhaps you feel that you are a disappointment to friends, loved ones, or others. You may feel pressure to be the best, to be perfect, or to behave in a particular way. You strive to live up to a perceived standard but find it difficult and stumble. As a result, you conclude that you can't live up to these expectations. That makes you feel terrible. As a way to punish yourself, you cut yourself. In your view, you deserve to suffer because you have essentially failed.

Lack of Self Worth/Feeling Unloved/Depression

One of the main reasons why people report cutting themselves is because they feel unloved or they lack a feeling of positive self-worth. Someone who does not feel good about themselves may feel that it hardly matters what happens to them. Cutting might be their way to quietly suffer.

For example, you might cut yourself because you don't feel good about yourself. You see yourself as having no value to others. You feel that no one loves you or cares about you. You begin to cut and things get worse. Now you feel like a "loser" for cutting. You are too ashamed to tell someone about how you feel or that you cut. You don't want others to see you as a "loser" so you keep the cutting behavior a secret. You're stuck, feeling alone, frightened, and trapped in a loop of shame, guilt, and self-injury. Cutting begets more cutting. Cutting because someone feels unloved or unworthy of being loved may also be a sign of depression.

Physical/Stress Release/Emotional Regulation

Some people are compelled to cut themselves because they are experiencing a great deal of emotional pain. Emotional pain can be difficult to tolerate. Physical pain is different than emotional pain and for some, it provides a stress release. It may even feel soothing. This release, however, is temporary because cutting doesn't solve any problems. It simply a perceived relief from one form of pain. It is pain but in a different form.

Some reports in the academic literature also say that seeing blood is an important element of cutting. For some, seeing the blood makes them feel calm. Some have even reported that it makes them feel alive. It may also be a sign that someone has cut themselves "correctly."

One study by Glenn & Klonsky (2010) found that approximately half of the study participants believed that it is important to see blood. Seeing blood helps the study participants to relieve tension and it made them feel calm. The researchers also noted that the individuals who felt that it was important to see blood during their self-cutting activities were also more likely to have symptoms consistent with borderline personality disorder and bulimia nervosa.

Emotional Numbness

Alternatively, some people have difficulty feeling emotions. This is often referred to as emotional numbness. To "feel" some people cut to feel something, anything. For some, experiencing pain is perceived as better than feeling nothing at all.

Attempting to Get Help

In some cases, people who cut themselves secretly hope that someone will see the physical marks on their body. Individuals who cut for this reason often have difficulty expressing what is bothering them. If someone sees these wounds, then they may realize how much suffering is taking place. In this way, the cutting may be an attempt to gain the attention of those around you. Individuals who realize that you are cutting may see this as your way of asking for help.

Lack of Coping Skills

Another major reason why some individuals cut themselves is that they were never taught how to properly deal with difficult situations. For instance, you get into a fight with your friend. You are angry at your friend but not sure how to handle the situation. You desperately want to solve the problem but don't know how to approach your friend. You don't know what to say. You were never taught or no one ever showed you how to properly express your feelings. Instead of talking to your friend and appropriately resolving the problem, your anger remains bottled up. To decrease your unpleasant angry feelings, you cut yourself. That may be all that you know how to do. In essence, you lack problem-solving skills. If someone has never been taught how to manage life problems or emotional difficulties then it makes sense that they would have difficulty appropriately dealing with stressful situations. Cutting may temporarily serve as a mechanism for handling life stresses but it is always a sign that something is wrong and that help is necessary.

In another instance, perhaps you are easily frustrated. The fact that you are easily frustrated may be a sign that you have a limited ability to tolerate challenging situations. That does not mean that something is wrong with you. It's simply a sign that, in all likelihood, no one ever modeled for you how to properly deal with these types of situations. The good news is that these skills can be learned very easily with the help of a therapist.

Cutting May Be Seen As "Cool" & Thus Is Contagious

You may have heard about a peer who cuts themselves. Perhaps you thought that it was a way to be "cool" and or that people who are considered "cool" engage in this type of behavior. If you never heard about cutting, then you may have never tried it. Since a peer who was perceived as being "cool" cuts, you want to try too. In that way, cutting may be seen as being contagious.

An Attempt To Establish Control

It is human nature to want to feel as though you are in control of your life. If someone's life is chaotic, to the point where they feel as though they have lost control, then they may attempt to establish some level of control in their lives. Cutting may be seen as a way to establish that control. For some people, cutting is akin to gaining power and control. Seeing marks on their skin may make them feel independent or feel different than other people. Unfortunately, gaining control through cutting is an illusion. Cutting may give someone the impression that they are in control but in reality, they are not. Cutting only serves to make their lives more chaotic and out of control.

Why You Should Not Cut

Cutting is dangerous. You might accidentally do more harm than you intended. It is simply not safe to purposely harm yourself.

Cutting is also an ineffective coping strategy. It may provide *temporary* relief but the emotional pain that motivated the cutting always returns. Nothing good comes from self-injury.

Also, cutting can leave permanent marks on the body.
People tend to cut themselves when they are experiencing negative emotions. These permanent marks or scars on the body can be painful reminders of those negative emotions. Think of cutting as akin to getting a bad tattoo that lasts forever. No one wants to be reminded of negativity.

Another reason why you should not cut is that there is help available. You don't have to suffer in silence. There are many effective treatments for cutting.

How To Receive Help For Cutting

To receive help, you need to let someone know you want to help. For teenagers or young adults, this can be especially difficult. They may not want to talk to their parents about seeing a therapist. They may also feel as though the parents would reject their suggestion for getting help.

Everyone's situation is different so it will be up to you to decide how to approach this. One thing is for certain: the fact that your cutting is a sign that something is wrong and that professional help is needed.

If you choose to talk to your parents, you don't necessarily have to reveal all the details about why you want to see a therapist. It may be enough to simply request that your parents take you to see a therapist.

If your parents are not willing to take you to a therapist for you, then you may want to consider a different approach. This can include discussing your dilemma with a mentor, an authority figure in your school, or ideally, someone you feel you may be able to assist you in convincing your parents to take you to a therapist. This individual may be able to speak to your parents on your behalf.

Some people find it helpful to write a letter to their parents about why they want help. Writing a letter is a different way of expressing yourself. Some people find it easier to express their feelings through words rather than through face-to-face communication. Do what's best for you given your situation.

There are many effective treatments for cutting. The best treatments include individual therapy. Some other treatments involve family therapy, depending on how willing your family is to being involved in your treatment. Medication can also be helpful. It could reduce your urge to cut and stabilize your mood. Emotional stability could lead to a decreased desire to cut.

Many people who cut feel as though they are alone. They may feel as though no one understands their situation. Nothing could be further from the truth. Millions of individuals are helped with therapy. You can be helped too. Asking for help is an essential first step in overcoming life problems. Do it. You deserve to be happy and with the right help, you can.

A Long-Term Solution: Therapy

If you have been cutting yourself or considering suicide, then it is important that you consult a mental health professional as soon as possible. If you have an immediate plan to end your life, then you should receive emergency attention. If you're having suicidal thoughts but do not have a plan, then now is the time that you should seek counseling.

A therapist can assist you in addressing your suicidal thoughts. They could analyze why you feel the way that you do and assist you in developing problem-solving skills. It is important to develop problem-solving skills because there are many problems throughout life. In the words of Viktor Frankl *"what never can be ruled out is the unavoidability of suffering."* We should expect problems as a part of life, we should learn to deal with them and perhaps even find meaning in them. Therapy can greatly assist you in this process.

If you gain the skills to deal with life problems, you will be much less apt to consider suicide. As we know, one possible reason for considering suicide is a lack of problem-solving skills. Having the right problem-solving skills is an essential life skill.

Many people are reluctant to seek professional help. Even those who have suffered for many years often don't see the value in seeing a therapist. Some hold the opinion that seeking professional help is a sign of weakness. They hold the distorted view that everyone should be able to solve their own problems. Others don't wish to share the intimate details of their life with a stranger. Unfortunately, those attitudes remain prevalent in our society and contribute to the millions of people who live with untreated mental illnesses. Studies consistently show that individuals willing to seek treatment have the greatest likelihood of success.

References

Glenn, C. R., & Klonsky, E. D. (2010). The role of seeing blood in non-suicidal self-injury. *Journal of Clinical Psychology, 66* (4), 466-473.

Chapter 4: How To Get Help

In An Emergency Situation

There are multiple ways to get help. Research shows that if there is a time delay between someone deciding that they want to end their lives and having access to the means to do it, they are less likely to commit the act. If you're feeling suicidal, call 911 or 988 or the local crisis team immediately. The trained emergency response staff can protect you.

Tell a friend, a family member, a mentor or a mental health professional that you're considering suicide. These individuals can act on your behalf and get you the help that you require.

Go to the hospital, if needed. At the hospital, you can speak to someone in the psychiatric emergency department. You will likely encounter nurses, social workers, and physicians. They can assist you in protecting yourself and getting you the help that you need.

Another option is to text (741741) or call the National Suicide Helpline. In the United States, they can be reached at 1-800-237-TALK (8255). You can speak with crisis intervention counselors 24 hours a day, seven days a week. They can assist you in getting you the help that you need.

Best Places To Find Help

12 Places To Find Free or Low-Cost Psychological Help

Compiled below is a list of possible free or lost cost assistance in your community. Free or low-cost services may not be easy to find but if you look hard enough you will likely find something (or someone) that works for you.

1. **Community Mental Health Centers (CMHCs).** Virtually every community has one. Generally, these services are provided to individuals who have Medicaid, Medicare, or another public aid program. If you do not have one of those insurance programs, the staff at CMHC can assist you in applying for them. Sometimes the cost of each service session is free depending on your financial situation. Sliding scale fees may be required. Outpatient services at CMHCs vary but most generally offer the following:

- Individual therapy
- Group therapy
- Couple counseling or marriage therapy
- Case management services
- Intensive case management services
- Housing support and transitional independence programs
- Medication management with a psychiatrist
- Foster care services
- Substance abuse services
- Support and advocacy
- Wraparound services

2. **NAMI Support Groups:** NAMI (the National Alliance On Mental Illness) is a large advocacy group that assists individuals with mental illnesses and family members who have individuals with mental illness. NAMI has support groups in virtually every city across the country. Many NAMI support group members are seasoned veterans. They understand and have dealt with the mental health system often because they have family members with mental illness. The support groups are free.

3. **AA/NA:** (Alcoholics Anonymous or Narcotics Anonymous.) AA or NA is described as a fellowship in which individuals who have difficulty with either drugs or alcohol share their experiences with others to help each other. Virtually every community has an AA or NA group. There is a distinction between open groups and

close groups but the meetings are always free and virtually everyone is welcome. AA is a wondrous organization that helped many people overcome their use of addictive substances.

4. **Grief Support Groups**: Many communities have grief support groups. They may be offered by community mental health centers or by local private therapists. Click here to find a list of grief support groups in your community.

5. **State and Local Health Department**: the state or the local health department does not provide free mental health services but they likely have a list of free services in your community. Contact the health department and explain your situation. Asked they connect you to free or low-cost services. They should be able to direct you to the proper assistance.

6. **University Research Centers:** Don't overlook university research centers. Many universities are researching psychotherapy or psychotropic medications. They are looking for participants that often they are willing to compensate you for your time. Those who are participating in university research often have access to cutting-edge treatments.

7. **Internet Therapy:** There are many websites in which clinicians are offering Internet therapy. Most often there is a cost for these services but depending on who you choose, the services may be very affordable. In many cases, Internet therapy may be cheaper than individual therapy.

8. **Veterans Administration (VA) Hospital**: Those to those served in the military, now or in the past, have access to free or low-cost services through the VA. Many of these treatments are evidence-based and cutting-edge. Click here to find access to local VA services.

9. **Church Counselors**: Members of the clergy often provide free or low-cost counseling to members of their church. It can be an excellent source of mental health and spiritual guidance.

10. **Salvation Army**: The Salvation Army is a community support organization that can provide mental health assistance for individuals in need. They specifically offer substance abuse services, community support connections for individuals with chronic and serious mental illness, and in some communities supportive housing. What each Salvation Army offers is dependent upon the community.

11. **University Counseling Centers**: Virtually all colleges and universities offer free or low-cost services to their students. Often these services are short-term in nature but highly effective. If a student requires more intensive or long-term treatment, the counseling center staff usually have developed partnerships with other therapists in the communities with whom they refer. College or counseling centers are often staff with a psychiatrist, social workers, and psychologist. Many provide psychiatric evaluations and medication management and assessment services.

12. **Employee Assistance Programs (EAPs):** Many employers offer EAPs. EAPs are short-term counseling programs in which an individual can receive limited treatment for problems such as depression, anxiety, emotional distress, relationship issues, or substance abuse problems. Employers who offer these programs do so free of charge. The personal information shared with EAP is strictly confidential. For those who need longer-term counseling, EAP counselors can refer you to someone in your community.

Final Word

Life might be difficult now but it will not always be this way. Millions of people have felt the way that you do at some point in their lives. They sought help, received help, and have now fully recovered. You can expect a similar, positive outcome if you are willing to seek help.